The 1619 Project
Born on the Water

by **Nikole Hannah-Jones** *and* **Renée Watson**

illustrated by **Nikkolas Smith**

Kokila

KOKILA

An imprint of Penguin Random House LLC, New York

First published in the United States of America by Kokila, an imprint of Penguin Random House LLC, 2021

Visit us online at penguinrandomhouse.com.

Library of Congress Cataloging-in-Publication Data is available.

Printed in the United States of America

ISBN 9780593307359

1 3 5 7 9 10 8 6 4 2

PC

Design by Jasmin Rubero
Text set in Dapifer Font Family

For Najya
–N. H. J.

For Caleb & Nehemiah
–R. W.

**To my son, Zion. May you continue on the path of bravery
and brilliance that your ancestors have laid before you.**
–N. S.

Questions

My teacher gives us an assignment. "Who are you?" she asks. "Trace your roots.
Draw a flag that represents your ancestral land."

Most of my classmates can count back many generations
and learn about the countries where their families came from.
They draw their flags. But I leave my paper blank.

I do not know where I begin, what my story is.

At home, Grandma asks, "How was school?"

I tell her about the assignment, how I couldn't finish it.
How I can only count back three generations, here, in this country—
where my parents, my grandparents, and my great-grandparents were born.
But before that, I do not know.

I tell her that I am ashamed.

Grandma gathers the whole family, says,
"Come, let me tell you our beginning.
Let me tell you where we're from."

What Grandma Tells Me

They say our people were born on the water,
but our people had a home, a place, a land
before they were sold.

400 years ago, in 1619, our ancestors were taken
and brought here on a ship called the *White Lion*
a whole year before the *Mayflower* arrived.

But before that dreadful voyage,
there was a time when they did not pray
for freedom.

There was a time when they did not sing
about overcoming.

Their story does not begin
with whips and chains.

They had a home, a place, a land,
a beginning.

Their story is our story.
Before they were
enslaved, they were
free.

They Had a Language

They spoke Kimbundu,
had their own words
for love
for friend
for family.

The Kingdom of Ndongo
was nestled between
the Lukala and the Kwanza Rivers
on a high, high plateau
in West Central Africa.

The people were good with their hands,
knew the power of a seed,
how to plant it, water it,
how to make something out of nothing.

The people were good with their minds,
good at math and science.
They used shells for money,
counting, recording, trading.
They knew what their work was worth.

They spoke Kimbundu,
had their own words
for joy
for grow
for home.

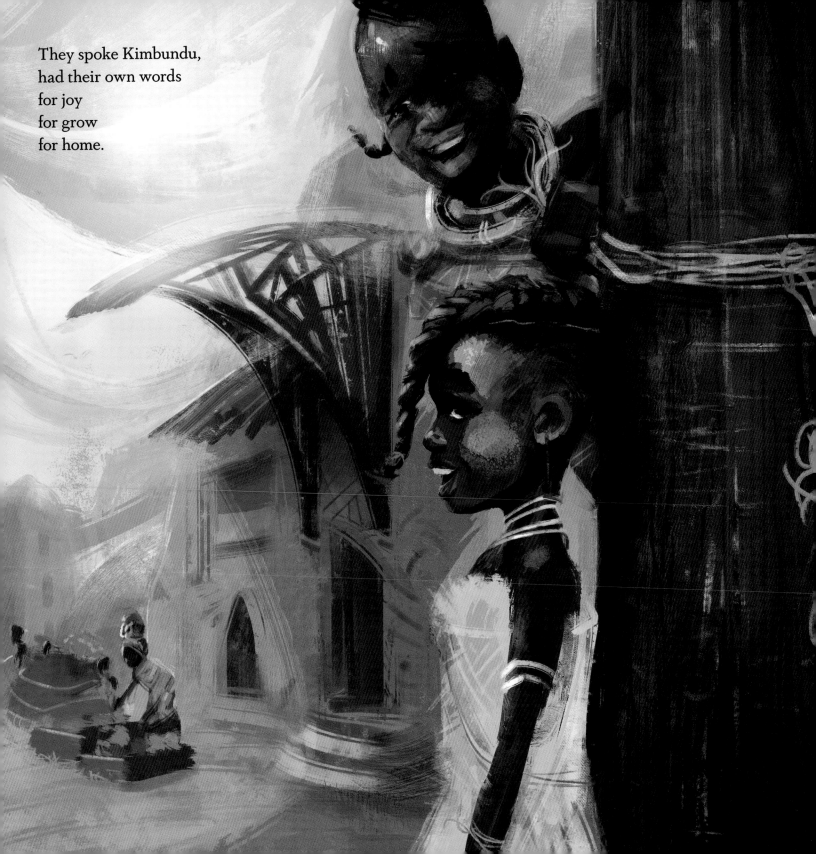

Their Hands Had a Knowing

Their hands had a knowing.
They knew how to hold a baby close,
how to rock the child to keep her from crying.

Their hands knew how to mix herbs,
how to get the just-right flavor for a meal.

Their hands knew how to beat
and twist and shape iron.
How to make gardening tools, armor, and weapons.

Their hearts had a knowing.
They knew how to make work joyful,
how to create rhythm by pounding the tools against metal,
knew how to make music to keep them company as they worked.

Their minds had a knowing,
worldly, curious, sharp.
When they met the white people,
they learned quick, taught their tongues
to speak Portuguese,
taught their eyes to read strange words.

They knew how to mix the old with the new,
how even an ancient people always had more to learn.

And They Danced

And the people moved their feet,
moved their whole bodies
to the melody of horns and stringed instruments,
of marimbas and drums.

They danced to celebrate, to mourn.
They danced as a way of worship, to offer thanks.

Their bodies a song under open sky and bright sun.
Their bodies a swaying testament to the beauty of creation.

Stolen

And the white people took them anyway.
Kidnapped them.
Baptized them in the name of their god.
Stamped them with new names.

Ours is no immigration story.

They did not get to pack bags stuffed
with cherished things, with the doll grandmama
had woven from tall grass,
with the baby blanket handed down
from generation to generation all the way back,
so far back that it carried the scent of the ancestors.

They could not hug their fathers and mothers,
daughters and sons,
hearts thumping in rhythm,
clinging to that final sweetness before the parting.
No promises, whispered from mouth to ear,
of seeing each other soon.

Just wails and sobs. Confusion and
wrists worn raw from shackles made of iron,
feet split and bloody from the 200-mile march
along the Kwanza River.

They had no things. But they had their minds.
The old ways, the harvest songs, the just-right mix of herbs
etched in their memories.

They had their bodies. Histories and bloodlines
and drums pulsing in their veins.
With trembling fingers
they braided seeds into their hair, defiantly hiding
tiny pieces of home
to plant one day
in new soils.

No matter what some say,
the people fought.

And the white people took them anyway.
Forced them into the bottom of an evil ship,
to sail to a "New World"
they had no desire to see.

Ours is no immigration story.

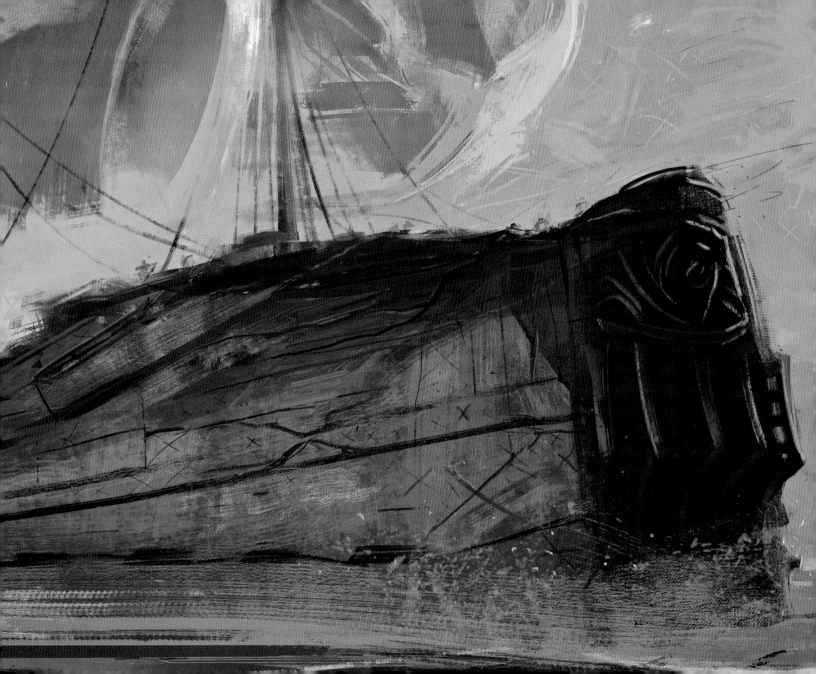

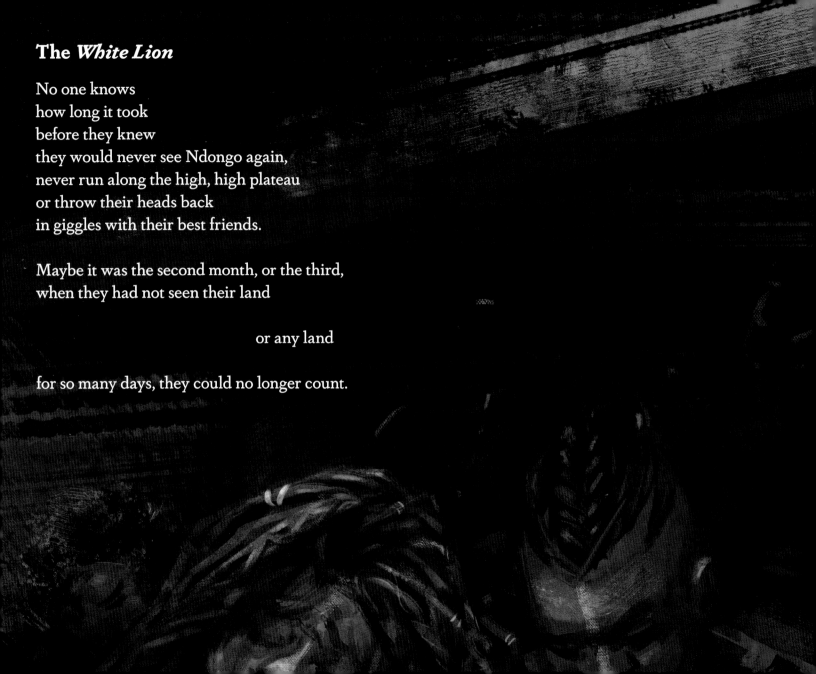

The *White Lion*

No one knows
how long it took
before they knew
they would never see Ndongo again,
never run along the high, high plateau
or throw their heads back
in giggles with their best friends.

Maybe it was the second month, or the third,
when they had not seen their land

                        or any land

for so many days, they could no longer count.

Some could not bear the pain.
They refused to eat.
They shut their mouths
until their hearts gave out.

Others tossed themselves
into the teal eternity of the Atlantic Ocean,
swimming one last time
with the ancestors.

Sickness and hunger,
filth and cruelty
took the others. Almost half.

But those who did not die
resolved to live
no matter what.

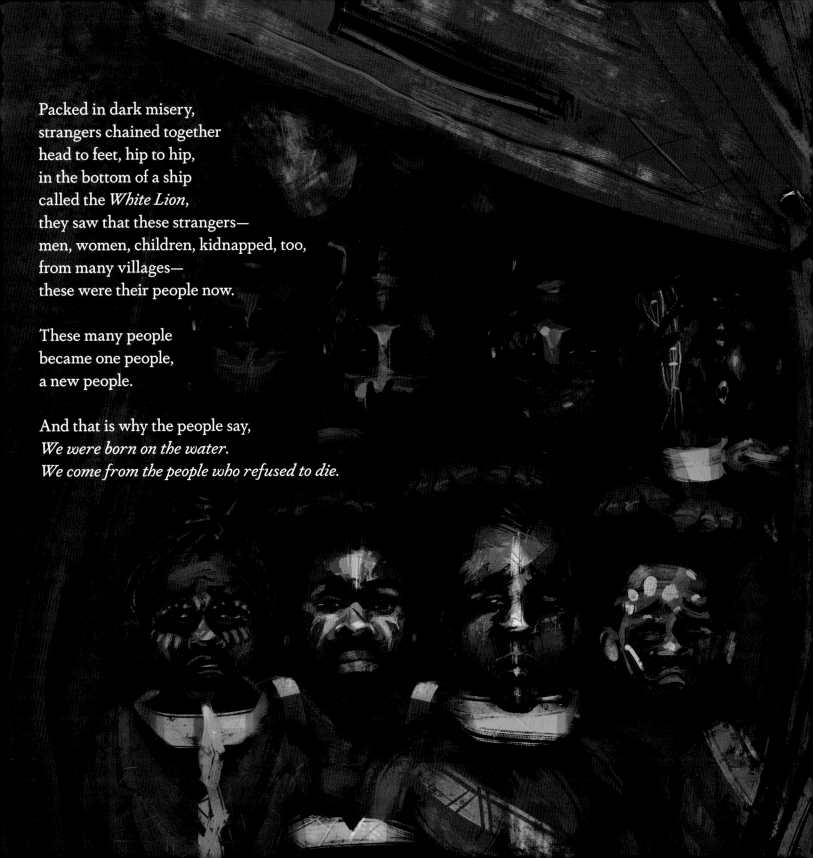

Packed in dark misery,
strangers chained together
head to feet, hip to hip,
in the bottom of a ship
called the *White Lion*,
they saw that these strangers—
men, women, children, kidnapped, too,
from many villages—
these were their people now.

These many people
became one people,
a new people.

And that is why the people say,
We were born on the water.
We come from the people who refused to die.

Point Comfort

Finally,
the ship stopped moving
and the people were dragged
to the deck.
They closed their eyes against the light
of a sun they had not seen
since Mother Africa's coast.
They closed their eyes against the sight
of a land that was not theirs.

They cried a silent cry
as white men spoke strange words
talking about their bodies
and with a handshake
traded another's child, another's momma and daddy,
20 to 30 beloved human beings in all,
for a few pounds of food and drink.

400 years ago,
in the year 1619,
the white people called this land Virginia,
a sweet-sounding word
for a place of such pain,
a sweet-sounding word for the place
where American slavery began.

Tobacco Fields

From sunup to sundown,
the people worked the fields,
growing and harvesting tobacco.
The crops were sold to Europe,
bringing wealth to Virginia,
but the enslaved people did not get anything
in return for their labor.

The people worked
and worked.

When the people grew weary,
they remembered their yesterdays,
remembered their songs from Ndongo,
sang them to ease their spirits.
As they sang, they looked into the future,
hoped for better days,
planted prayers into the heavens,
praying, praying, praying
for freedom.

How to Make a Home

After a long day's work planting tobacco in the fields,
after brutal treatment, after nothing to show for their hard work,
sadness would come, a longing for Ndongo,
for the mommas, for the daddies, for the friends
they could no longer hug and talk with under the warm sun.

We are in a strange land, they said.
But we are here and we will make this home.
We have our songs, our recipes, our know-how.
We have our joy. We will love, laugh, sing,
and hug our children as tight as you can hold a child.
We will survive because we have each other.

And so the people
planted the seeds they'd carried over the ocean,
snuck to visit one another in the dark of night,
sang songs, swapped tales of yesterday,
remembering, remembering.

And the people planted dreams and hope,
willed themselves to keep
living, living.

And the people learned new words
for love
for friend
for family

for joy
for grow
for home.

We are in a strange land, they said.
But we are here and we will make this home.
We have determination, imagination, faith.
We will survive because we have each other.

The Tuckers of Tidewater, Virginia

1624.
Anthony and Isabella,
enslaved on the plantation
of Captain William Tucker
and his wife, Mary Tucker.

Two ordinary people
forced to till the soil,
forced to build a country
they were not from

found a way to build
a love for each other,
to marry and create
a family, a legacy.

They did not know
their family would be
the start of a new people.

They were just two ordinary people
who had a son,
a new beginning,
a promise
to live on and on.

William Tucker

Hope is a promise.
Faith that a better day will come.
Belief that things will not always be this way.
Hope is refusal to give up, to die out.

Hope is a child born.

Way back then, hope had a name.
William Tucker.

He was born to ordinary people,
a man and a woman
who were not free
but who believed in freedom,
who were not free
but who believed
that one day
freedom would come
even if they never saw it.

These two ordinary people gave life
to an extraordinary child.
A child not of Africa,
a child not of Europe,
nor of the Native peoples already here.
But a child of the new people formed on the water.

The first Black child born in the land
that would become the United States.
The first truly American child.

Resist

Life was hard,
and it would get harder
for the generations to come.

White people told the people they were not human.
That the people were things
to be bought and sold and given as gifts
alongside horses and chairs.

When the people were beaten,
they said the people did not feel pain.
When they sold the people's children,
they said the people didn't love.
These were lies they made up
so they could feel okay
about slavery. It is wrong, always
and forever, to own human beings.
It is wrong, always and forever, to treat
human beings like things.

The people fought back.
For 250 years,
the people resisted every day
in ways big and small.
For 250 years,
the biggest resistance of all
was that the people kept living.

Legacy

And the people who were born on the water survived.
Kept living and living.

It was illegal to teach enslaved people how to read,
but they birthed generations of
teachers and librarians,
scholars and authors.

They were brokenhearted, beaten, and bruised,
but they became healers,
pastors and activists,
doctors and counselors.

No one could steal the people's joy.
They wrote songs,
created jazz and hip-hop,
rhythm and blues.

They became
inventors and athletes,
nurses and cooks,
pilots and architects,
farmers and housekeepers,
singers and artists,
dancers and poets,
mathematicians and scientists.

They passed on their stories
through the stitch of a quilt,
shared secret messages through songs.

The people survived.
The people fought.

And because the people survived
and because the people fought,
they finally got freedom.

And because the people survived
and because the people fought,
America has equality in the law.

And because the people survived
and because the people fought,
America began to live up to its promise of democracy.

It is the people who fight for this democracy still.

Pride

Grandma looks at me and my brother, tells us,
"This is why we say
Black Lives Matter,
why we celebrate Black Girl Magic,
why we believe we are our ancestors' wildest dreams.

"Never forget
we are their hope.

"Never forget you come from a people
of great strength," Grandma says.
"Be proud of our story, your story."

The next day, I go to school,
pull out my red crayon, my blue, and my white.
I draw the stars and I draw the stripes
of the flag of the country that my ancestors built,
that my grandma and grandpa built,
that I will help build, too.

And I am not ashamed.
I know what my story is,
where I am from,

where I begin . . .

Authors' and Illustrator's Notes

Our hope for *Born on the Water* is to show that Black Americans have their own proud origin story, one that did not begin in slavery, in struggle, and in strife but that bridges the gap between Africa and the United States of America. We begin this book with the rich cultures of West Africa and then weave the tale of how after the Middle Passage, Black Americans created a new people here on this land. We see these verses as snapshots of the Black American experience. Each poem is its own container for the intense emotions that are sometimes joyful, sometimes painful. We hope all young people who read this book are inspired to ask questions about where they are from and to learn their own origin stories. We especially hope Black American children who may be longing to feel connected to their roots come away empowered by the knowledge that there is no shame in descending from American slavery, and with the understanding that they come from a resilient people who loved, resisted, and persevered.

—Nikole Hannah-Jones & Renée Watson

Each beautiful poem that Nikole and Renée have crafted has its own energy. My goal in illustrating this book was to read, feel, internalize, and respond with a painting to match the vibe of each poem. Some illustrations have a more vibrant energy, some more chaotic and messy, some more peaceful, with smooth strokes: a visual representation of the infectious joy, heartbreaking struggles, and triumphant legacy of my ancestors. Countless Black Americans and I share this ancestral lineage, and often without any specifics, so I decided to illustrate a broad range of Central West African details, from architecture to hairstyles, instruments, and clothing.

I have also filled the book with African scarification pattern motifs, where Life, Death, and Rebirth are present. I am a Houston, Texas–born descendant of masterfully skilled, brilliant, and strong-willed survivors who were violently taken from West Central Africa and enslaved.

I paint these poems for them, as a manifestation of their wildest dreams come true.

—Nikkolas Smith

Visit 1619books.com for educator materials.